Movement Plus Rhymes, Songs, & Singing Games

*Other movement and dance materials
by Phyllis S. Weikart**

BOOKS

Movement Plus Music: Activities for Children Ages 3 to 7
Round the Circle: Key Experiences in Movement for Children
Teaching Movement & Dance: A Sequential Approach
Teaching Movement & Dance: Intermediate Folk Dance

RECORD/CASSETTE SERIES

Rhythmically Moving 1–9
(nine-record series, also available in cassettes)
Changing Directions 1–3
(three-record series, also available in cassettes)

VIDEOTAPE

Fitness Over 50

Note: The *Rhythmically Moving 1–9* series of records/cassettes contains the music for the movement activities presented in *Round the Circle* and *Teaching Movement & Dance: A Sequential Approach.* The *Rhythmically Moving 1–4* records/cassettes contain the music for activities described in *Movement Plus Music.* The *Changing Directions* series of records/cassettes contains the music for the folk dances described in *Teaching Movement & Dance: Intermediate Folk Dance.*

*Available from the High/Scope Press, 600 North River Street,
Ypsilanti, Michigan 48198, (313) 485-2000.

HIGH/SCOPE PRESS
A division of the
High/Scope Educational Research Foundation
600 North River Street, Ypsilanti, Michigan 48198

Movement Plus Rhymes, Songs, & Singing Games

Activities for Children Ages 3 to 7

Phyllis S. Weikart

*High/Scope Movement and Dance Consultant
Associate Professor, Division of Physical Education
The University of Michigan*

with

**Jane Allman
Elizabeth Carlton
Judith Cole
Valerie Johnson
Penny Mahoney
Claudia Spring
Carol Kolonay-Spangler**

*Endorsed Trainers in Phyllis S. Weikart's
Rhythmic Movement and Folk Dance Curriculum*

HIGH/SCOPE PRESS

Published by
THE HIGH/SCOPE PRESS

A division of the
High/Scope Educational Research Foundation
600 North River Street
Ypsilanti, Michigan 48198
(313) 485-2000

Library of Congress Cataloging in Publication Data: LC 88-751755

ISBN 0-931114-75-6

Printed in the United States of America

Contents

Singing Games 79

Preface

*T*his booklet should be viewed as a supplement to *Round the Circle: Key Experiences in Movement for Children.* It corresponds to my other activity booklet, *Movement Plus Music: Activities for Children Ages 3 to 7.*

The rhymes, action songs, and singing games presented here are founded on the eight key experiences I introduced in *Round the Circle:* (1) following movement directions, (2) describing movement (using language), (3) moving the body in non-locomotor ways, (4) moving the body in locomotor ways, (5) moving with objects, (6) expressing creativity in movement, (7) feeling and expressing beat, and (8) moving with others to a common beat. These key experiences introduce children to a wide range of developmentally appropriate movements, enabling them to practice movement skills that are very important in their development. These skills should be mastered by the age of seven.

I have written this booklet with assistance from seven trainers who are endorsed in my Rhythmic Movement and Folk Dance Curriculum. The booklet responds to the numerous requests we have received from our workshop participants for developmentally appropriate lead-up movements for the simple rhymes, action songs, and singing games enjoyed by children in preschool, kindergarten, and first grade. Our hope is that teachers, caregivers, and parents of young children will find it to be a useful addition to their movement and music collections.

I am deeply indebted to trainers Jane Allman, Wyandotte, MI; Elizabeth Carlton, Salisbury, NC; Judith Cole, Corpus Christi, TX; Valerie Johnson, Olympia, WA; Penny Mahoney, Beeville, TX; Claudia Spring, Pontiac, MI; and Carol Kolonay-Spangler, Bridgeport, CT, for their help with this project.

Phyllis S. Weikart

How to Use This Booklet

*T*he activities in this booklet are divided into three activity categories: (1) rhymes, (2) action songs, and (3) singing games. The age-range most appropriate for each activity is specified, but by making minor modifications in the movements, you can use any of the activities successfully with the entire age-range (3–7, preschool through first grade).

We have altered some of the rhymes, action songs, and singing games to accommodate large groups of children or to give children more opportunities to be the leader. In a few instances, the words for an activity have also been changed to be more understandable for today's children. Once the children are comfortable with an activity as we give it, you may wish to introduce the original version.

We recommend that you do the following to become familiar with each activity:

1. Note the intended age-range, which is listed at the top of each activity, and make whatever modifications might be necessary for your particular group of children.

2. In the activity description, review the Equipment and Formation sections, which identify the setting and any equipment that might be needed. Make sure you have enough equipment for each child and that your activity area is large enough to accommodate the movements.

3. Read through the Procedure section, so you understand the movement sequence thoroughly before you present it to the children.

The Teaching Model

The recommended method for presenting the movement sequences incorporates three basic concepts: **separate, simplify, facilitate.**

Separate. When presenting a movement, separate your spoken and visual presentations; in other words, separate your talk from your actions. Avoid describing while demonstrating, or demonstrating while describing. For example, to present an arm movement, ask the children to watch your arms and to do what you do, but do not talk while actually demonstrating the movement. Also, when presenting a new activity, introduce the movement sequence, or each segment of the sequence, *before* adding the words or tune for that sequence or segment. Your goal is to assure that each child will perform the movement successfully, with self-confidence and enjoyment. For new activities, progressing silently through the movement sequence first is easier for children than trying to learn the words or tune *and* the movements simultaneously. This process of learning movements first, and words or tune second, strengthens children's perceptions of the movement activities.

Simplify. You can simplify a sequence of movements by presenting one movement at a time. For example, if the movement calls for putting arms in front of the body and then behind the back, as in *Hokey Pokey,* put your arms in front of your body and then pause to give the children a chance to copy your movement. Next, put your arms behind your back, pausing again to give the children a chance to copy your movement. Finally, do the two movements in sequence. When all the children seem to be comfortable with the sequence, start labeling the movements by saying "Put your arms IN." Pause. "Now put them OUT."

Facilitate. Once the children have watched your demonstration or have performed a movement, help them develop an awareness of the movement by asking such questions as "Where did you put your arms first? Then where did you put them?" Children should be active participants in the learning process and, by asking these and similar questions, you will assure that they are.

Teaching Strategies*

- At first, select activities that involve just a few movements. Also, try to use rhymes or songs with simple movements first. And select rhymes or songs in which the children stay in their own space rather than those in which children move about the designated activity area.

- In presenting a movement sequence, do not expect the children to understand the directions "right" and "left" or require children to do the mirror-image of your movement. These skills are more appropriate for older children (second grade and above).

- Add the rhyme or song (or phrases of the rhyme or song) only after all the children fully understand how to do the movement.

- When practicing the movement sequence, use the same tempo that you plan to use for the rhyme or song.

- Avoid creating too fast a tempo for the rhyme or song, because the children may find it difficult to keep up with the movements.

---

*For a complete description of teaching strategies for presenting movement activities to young children, please refer to *Round the Circle: Key Experiences in Movement for Children,* which is available from the High/Scope Press.

- If a child is the leader as you go through a movement sequence, match the tempo of the chant or song to the child's tempo as you and the children sing or chant the rhyme together to accompany the movement.

- While doing a chant or song, pause intermittently to allow the children to finish executing the movements.

Rhymes

Bubble Gum

Bubble gum, bubble gum in a dish,
How many pieces do you wish?
1, 2, 3, . . . , POP!

Category

Rhyme

Age

5 – 7

Equipment

None.

Formation

Ask the children to stand so they are spread out about the area.

Procedure

Have the children practice bouncing in place to the beat of the first two lines of the rhyme. After a while, ask a child "How many pieces do you wish?" Suppose Carol answers and says, "Three." Suggest that Carol pick a movement she would like all the children to do as they count to three. For example, if Carol chooses a jump, the children will count and jump three times. On the word "POP," all the children should "freeze" into statue shapes.

Jack and Jill

Jack and Jill went up the hill
To fetch a pail of water.
Jack fell down and broke his crown,
And Jill came tumbling after.

Category

Rhyme

Age

3 – 5

Equipment

None.

Formation

Ask the children to spread out about the area. Each child should be standing on a small mat for tumbling (or several children should stand on a large mat).

Procedure

Start by suggesting that the children explore how they would climb up a hill, such as a hill near home. As they pretend to climb, ask them questions about how they are moving. Next, ask the boys to show how they would fall down the hill. Then ask the girls to show how they would fall down the hill. Remind the children to be careful as they practice falling. Then, do the whole sequence: Have all the children climb the hill, then ask the boys to fall down the hill, and then ask the girls to do so. Finally, say the nursery rhyme as the children act it out.

Variation

Ask two children to act out the rhyme. Substitute their names for "Jack" and "Jill."

Jack Be Nimble

Jack be nimble, Jack be quick,
Jack jump over the candlestick, JUMP!

Category

Rhyme

Age

4 – 7

Equipment

For each child, an object, such as a block, should be provided to represent a candlestick. The object should be easy to jump over.

Formation

Have the children stand so they are spread out about the area, and give each of them a "candlestick."

Procedure

Start by having the children practice jumping over their objects. Next, ask them to bounce to the beat of the rhyme. Practice these moves for a while. Finally, tell the children to jump over their "candlesticks" on the last word "JUMP."

Variations

● Change the words as follows:
Jack be nimble, Jack be quick,
Jack go around the candlestick, WALK, WALK, . . .
Have the children walk around their objects. Ask for a volunteer to find a special way to "go around the candlestick." Recite the rhyme, using the volunteer's name and method.

● Tie a rope between two objects and have the children go under it, using the following variation:

> *Jack be nimble, Jack be fine,*
> *Jack walk under the clothesline.*

● Using the following modification, ask the children to "freeze" into statues at the end of the rhyme:

> *Jack can wiggle, Jack can shake,*
> *Jack can show us a shape to make.*

Little Jack Horner

Little Jack Horner sat in a corner,
Eating a Christmas pie.
He put in his thumb, and pulled out a plum,
And said, "What a good boy am I!"

Category

Rhyme

Age

3–5

Equipment

None.

Formation

Ask the children to sit in an informal circle.

Procedure

Begin by reciting the first two lines of the rhyme and then ask "Can you pretend to be very little like Jack Horner?" After the children respond, ask "What did you do to make yourselves little?" Then recite the first two lines again and ask "What was Jack Horner doing?" After the children respond, ask them to pretend to eat pie. Next, act out the first two lines of the rhyme with them as you say the words.

Make a fist with your thumb sticking out and ask "Can you make one of your hands look like mine?" After the children have made fists like yours, start turning your thumb down and then up. Then recite the third and fourth lines of the rhyme and act out the sequence of actions, asking the children to join in. Finally recite the entire rhyme as you all act out the sequence of movements.

One, Two, Tie My Shoe

One, two, tie my shoe;
Three, four, shut the door;
Five, six, pick up sticks;
Seven, eight, lay them straight;
Nine, ten, start again!

Category

Rhyme

Age

4 – 7

Equipment

Two rhythm sticks per child. (Chopsticks or drinking straws may be substituted.)

Formation

Ask the children to sit so they are spread out about the area.

Procedure

The children should already be familiar with tapping body parts with sticks. Start this action by showing them how to tap the sticks on the floor; do this several times and then tap your shoulders with the sticks several times, asking the children to copy your movements. Next, use SAY & DO by tapping the floor two times and then tapping your shoulders two times, while you say "FLOOR, FLOOR, SHOULDERS, SHOULDERS." Then have the children try to do the movements. Ask the children if they know how many times you tapped the floor and how many times you tapped your shoulders. Recite the rhyme, tapping the floor two times and the shoulders two times for each line of the rhyme. The next time, ask for a volunteer to be the leader and to tap two places. As the volunteer taps, encourage the other children to match the volunteer's actions with words. Then ask them to join in the movements, using SAY & DO. Once the beat and motions are well established, recite the rhyme again. As the children develop more skill, have them try one tap at a time to each location (such as FLOOR, SHOULDERS), and continue through the sequence as described.

Ride a Fast Horse

Ride a fast horse to Banbury Cross,
To see a fine lady upon a white horse;
Rings on her fingers and bells on her toes,
She shall have music wherever she goes.

Category

Rhyme

Age

3 – 5

Equipment

None.

Formation

Seat the children in an informal circle.

Procedure

Start by asking the children to pretend they are sitting and riding on a horse, and talk about their movements as they do them. Next, recite the first two lines of the nursery rhyme. Then ask the children these questions: "Can you wiggle your fingers in front of you? Can you wiggle your toes in your shoes? Can you wiggle your fingers and toes? Let's see you pretend to ride the horse again." Now, together with the children, sequence all of the movements as you recite the entire nursery rhyme. Say each line slowly enough to give the children time to complete the sequence.

Rub-a-Dub-Dub

Rub-a-dub-dub,
We sit in a tub,
To give ourselves a bath.

We wash our feet (pause),
We wash our legs (pause),
As we give ourselves a bath.

Category

Rhyme (traditional words changed)

Age

3 – 7

Equipment

A hula hoop for each child.

Formation

Ask the children to spread out about the area and to sit inside their hula hoops.

Procedure

Begin by saying "Let's pretend that we are sitting in the bathtub taking a bath. What shall we wash first? John says we should wash our feet, and Sally says we should wash our legs. John, show us how we wash our feet. Sally, show us how to wash our legs. Let's all practice. Now listen to what I say, and when you hear the words 'feet' and 'legs,' pretend to wash them." Repeat the rhyme and ask the children to choose other parts to wash.

Variation

The chant may be further altered as follows:

Rub-a-dub-dub,
We get out of the tub,
Because we have finished our bath.

We dry our feet (pause),
We dry our legs (pause),
Because we have finished our bath.

When using this version, have the children practice moving out of the hoop to dry their feet and legs *before* you say the rhyme, as in the initial activity.

Sally Go Round the Sun

Sally go round the sun.
Sally go round the moon.
Sally go round the chimney pot
Every afternoon. BOOM!

Category

Rhyme

Age

3 – 7

Equipment

None.

Formation

Have the children sit in an informal circle.

Procedure

One child should choose a special way to walk around the inside of the circle. Substitute that child's name for "Sally," and start the rhyme to the child's walking beat. The other children should find a way to keep the beat in their seated position. On "BOOM," the child who is the leader should "freeze" in a statue shape, and the other children should copy the statue. Then ask a new child to volunteer to be the leader, and repeat the rhyme.

Variation

All the children can move at the same time. All should "freeze" and make a statue on "BOOM."

Two Little Dickey Birds

Two little dickey birds sitting on a wall,
One named Peter, the other named Paul.
Fly away, Peter. Fly away, Paul.
Come back, Peter. Come back, Paul

Category

Rhyme (modified actions)

Age

3 – 7

Equipment

One large block and one carpet square for each child.

Formation

Place each large block on a carpet square, spreading them all about the area. Ask each child to sit on one of the blocks. The blocks will serve as the children's "walls."

Procedure

Begin by asking "Can you move your arms and pretend to fly? What are you doing with your arms to pretend flying?" Next ask "Can you fly like a bird around the room without touching any other bird?" Pause while the children move about. Then ask "What did you do with your legs when you flew?" Allow the children enough time to explore flying. Then say "I want you to listen to a rhyme. When you hear the words 'fly away,' make up your own way to fly around the room. When you hear the words 'come back,' make up your own way to come back to your block."

Talk about these two sets of action words for a while, so the children become familiar with them. Finally recite the rhyme and have the children act it out.

Variation

You can also do this activity with two child volunteers (to be Peter and Paul). Instead of using "Peter" and "Paul," use names of the volunteers.

Two Little Sausages

Two little sausages, Frying in a pan;
One went POP, And the other went BAM!

Category

Rhyme

Age

3 – 7

Equipment

A paper plate and two rhythm sticks for each child. (Chopsticks or drinking straws may be substituted for the rhythm sticks.)

Formation

Seat the children on the floor in an informal circle, with one paper plate in front of each child. Each child should be holding two rhythm sticks.

Procedure

Suggest that the children explore tapping the beat on the paper plates with both sticks at the same time, or with one stick and then with the other stick. Then ask "Who would like to be the leader and show us how to tap?" As the volunteer taps, have the other children join in the tapping movement, using the same beat. Finally, you can recite the rhyme to the beat the children are using.

Next touch your shoulders with the ends of the sticks and say "Can you make your sticks do what mine are doing? Can you find another place on your body to touch with the sticks? When you hear me say 'BAM,' touch your sticks on the place you have chosen and 'freeze.' " Then repeat the rhyme and have the children join in, tapping the beat on the plates with their sticks. When they hear "BAM," they should "freeze" the sticks in whatever location they have chosen.

Variation

Ask the children to select two different body parts, one to tap on the word "POP" and one to tap on the word "BAM." Tap the beat on plates only for the first two lines of the rhyme, up to the word "pan," and then add the body taps on the words "POP" and "BAM."

Wee Willie Winkie

Wee Willie Winkie runs through the town,
Upstairs (pause), and downstairs (pause),
In his nightgown,
He knocks at the window,
He calls through the lock,
Are all the children in their beds?
It's past eight o'clock!

Category

Rhyme (modified)

Age

3 – 7

Equipment

None.

Formation

Ask the children to stand or to sit in an informal circle.

Procedure

Ask the children to run in place if they are standing or to make their arms "run" if they are seated. An alternative movement might be to have the children lie on their backs and make their legs "run" in the air. Ask "Can you pretend that you are running upstairs? Downstairs? What did you do to show you were going upstairs and downstairs?" At this point, help the children recall the sequence of running in place, pretending to go upstairs, and pretending to go downstairs. You might choose to recite the first three lines of the nursery rhyme while the children are doing associated movements.

Next, recite the fourth line and talk with the children about knocking at the window: "If you were knocking at the window, how would you do it? Since the window is glass, would your knock be hard or soft?" Once the children have demonstrated how they would knock at the window, ask them how they would call through the lock. Then recite the last two lines of the rhyme and ask the children how they would go to sleep in their beds. Have them talk about their positions. Finally, do the entire rhyme with the actions.

17

Action Songs

Barnacle Bill

Category

Action song

Age

3 – 7

Equipment

None.

Formation

Ask the children to sit in a circle.

Procedure

Begin by telling the children that you are going to sing them a song that names a certain body part. Sing the song. Now that the children know the song is about thumbs, ask them to explore ways to move both their thumbs. Now sing the song again, asking the children to keep the beat with their thumb motions.

Sing the second verse to the children to introduce the next movement. Suggest that the children pat their shoes first with both hands and next with one hand and then with the other as you sing the verse again.

Follow the same procedure in singing the third verse, having the children practice patting their knees.

Variation

Challenge older children to find a place to pat that rhymes with the numbers used in the song.

Barnacle Bill

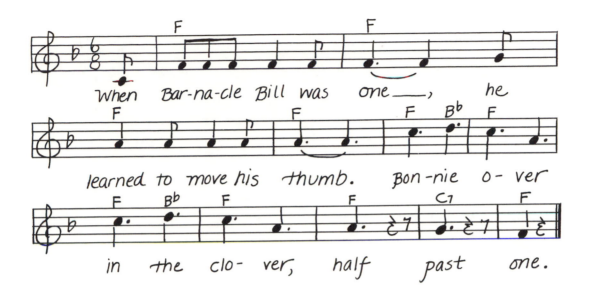

When Bar-na-cle Bill was one ___, he learned to move his thumb. Bon-nie o-ver in the clo-ver, half past one.

Verse 2: When Barnacle Bill was two,
           he learned to pat his shoes...
Verse 3: When Barnacle Bill was three,
           he learned to pat his knees...
Verse 4: When Barnacle Bill was four,
           he learned to pat the floor...
Verse 5: When Barnacle Bill was five,
           he learned to pat his thighs...

The Bear Climbed Up the Mountain
(The Bear Went Over the Mountain)

Category

Action Song

Age

3 – 7

Equipment

None.

Formation

Ask the children to stand so they are spread out in the activity area.

Procedure

Begin by asking the children to explore various ways to move about the room. As they do this, ask them to describe the ways they are moving. Ask some of the children to demonstrate their movements for the other children.

Then say "Let's pretend that we are bears climbing up a mountain. How would we climb the mountain if we were bears in a zoo?" Once the children get started, add the song. When you sing "to see what he could see," pretend to be looking around.

Variations

• Substitute another animal for the bear, such as a rabbit, bird, or snake, and change "climbed" to "hopped" (for the rabbit), or "flew" (for the bird), or "slithered" (for the snake).

• Ask a child to choose how to move, then incorporate the movement in your song: "Climb the mountain with Penny (3 times), and then we pat (shake, wiggle, sway) the beat. And then we pat the beat (2 times). Climb the mountain with Penny (3 times), and then we pat the beat."

The Bear Climbed Up the Mountain

Oh, the bear climbed up the moun- tain, the bear climbed up the moun- tain, the bear climbed up the moun- tain to see what he could see. To see what he could see, To see what he could see. Oh the bear climbed up the moun- tain to see what he could see.

Beat Is Steady
(Are You Sleeping?)

Category

Action song

Age

3 – 7

Equipment

None.

Formation

Have the children sit in an informal circle.

Procedure

Begin by patting the beat on your head and ask the children to copy what you are doing. As you achieve a common tempo, start singing the song. Say "Who has another idea about where we can pat the beat? Carol is patting the beat on the floor. Let's all try that." Now, sing the song to Carol's beat. Follow the same procedure with other children's ideas.

Next, begin to pat a slow beat on your knees and say "Am I patting slowly or quickly? Can you pat slowly with me? Can we rock back and forth to our slow beat?" Once the children have mastered the movement, start singing the song. The underlined words and syllables in the song will help you set the beat for the rocking movement. Encourage the children to find new ways to move to the slow beat as you sing the song.

Variations

• The children can use teddy bears, other stuffed toys, or dolls to pat or to rock with the beat.

• Two children can sit together inside a hula hoop and rock to the slow beat.

• Two children can hold the ends of a rhythm stick and move the stick together on the slow beat (for example, they might raise and lower it). Try to pair children who need help responding to the beat with those who respond more accurately to the beat. Sing slowly, so the children have enough time to respond to the beat with their movements.

Beat Is Steady

Christmas Time (Winter Time) Is Here

(Jimmy Crack Corn)

Category

Action song

Age

3 – 7

Equipment

Two sleigh bells per child. *Note.* If you do not have enough bells, or if you wish to do the song at a time other than the Christmas holidays, substitute the word "hands" for the word "bells."

Formation

Ask the children to stand or sit in a circle.

Procedure

Encourage the children to explore a bell-ringing (shaking) motion with their hands. Begin to shake your hands in front of your body and say "I can shake my hands in front of me. Can you do that? Where else can you shake your hands?" As the children shake their hands in different ways, focus on one particular child and say "Where were you shaking your hands, Johnny?" Then ask other children to describe their shaking motions.

When all the children seem comfortable with the shaking motion, give them each sleigh bells for each hand. Ask a child who is shaking his or her bells up high to be the leader. As the child begins the movement, you can start singing the song. After this, choose another child who is shaking the bells in a different position to lead next, and sing the song with words that describe this child's motions. For example, the song could be "Shake those bells in front of you."

Variation

Ask children to do other movements, and adapt the song accordingly. One example might be "Pat your chin with both your hands (repeated three times), as we all keep the beat."

Christmas Time (Winter Time) Is Here

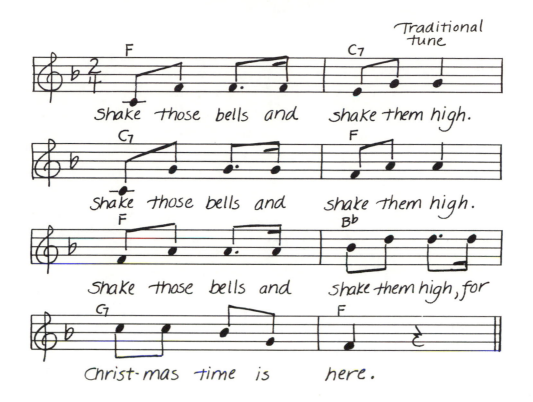

Traditional tune

Shake those bells and shake them high.

Shake those bells and shake them high.

Shake those bells and shake them high, for

Christ-mas time is here.

The Cookie Man
(The Muffin Man)

Category

Action song

Age

3 – 7

Equipment

One carpet square per child, if desired.

Formation

Ask the children to spread out about the area. Each child should sit next to a carpet square, if possible.

Procedure

Begin by saying "Today let's pretend that we are making cookies. What kind of cookies shall we bake today?" (This activity would be a good follow-up to the actual experience of making cookies.) Once you decide what kind of cookies you will pretend to make, sing Verse 1 of the song. Then ask the children such questions as "What do we do first when we make cookies? That's right Jeffrey, we get out the bowl and all the things we are going to use. Now let's pretend to put sugar, butter, and eggs in the bowl. After we add these ingredients, what do we do? Libby is showing us how we stir the cookie mix. Let's all stir our cookie dough. When we get it all stirred up, what do we do next? Yes, we roll out the dough. How do we roll out the dough? Let's pretend to roll out the dough on our carpet square. Can you make a cookie shape on your dough? What shape are you making? Can you make another shape? What do we do after we cut out the shapes? That's right, Judy, we put them on trays and put them in the oven to bake."

   Once you have gone through the make-believe cookie-baking exercise, suggest that the children listen carefully to the song and that they try to do what the words say.

The Cookie Man

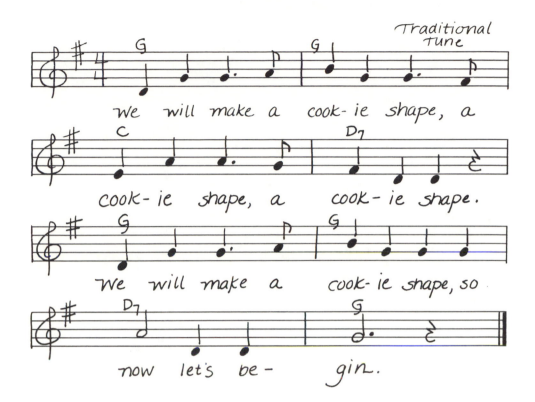

Traditional Tune

We will make a cook-ie shape, a cook-ie shape, a cook-ie shape. We will make a cook-ie shape, so now let's be-gin.

Verse 2: We will stir our cookie dough...
and then we'll roll it out.
Verse 3: We'll roll out the cookie dough...
and then we'll cut the shapes.
Verse 4: We will make a cookie shape...
and then we'll bake our cookies.
Verse 5: We will eat our cookies up...
until they're all gone.

Do as I'm Doing

Category

Action song

Age

3 – 7

Equipment

A carpet square for each child.

Formation

Ask the children to stand scattered about the area, with each child on a carpet square.

Procedure

Suggest that the children explore various nonlocomotor movements, such as bending and straightening, pushing and pulling, and patting various body parts as they stand on their carpet squares. After they have explored these movements for a while, ask for a volunteer to demonstrate a movement. As the other children copy the volunteer's movement, talk about what they are doing. Now, encourage the children to do the movement together to a steady beat, and then begin the song, fitting the tempo to their group beat. Adapt the song's tempo in this way for each new movement demonstrated by your volunteers.

Variation

You could also have the children work with a hula hoop, in pairs, with one child demonstrating a movement and the other copying it. (This partner variation is suitable for older children or for younger children who are experienced with the activity.) To begin this activity, you should start singing the song. Working with a partner, a child stands inside a hula hoop and performs a movement that the partner outside the hoop copies. The partners then switch places and roles, as you continue singing. Each time you stop singing, have the children who are copying recall the movement they did. Before you begin singing again, the children who will be leaders next should plan the movements they will do.

Do as I'm Doing

Do as I'm do-ing, Fol-low, fol-low me!

Do as I'm do-ing, Fol-low, fol-low me!

If I do it high or low, If I do it fast or slow,

Do as I'm do-ing, Fol-low, fol-low me!

Do as I'm do-ing, Fol-low, fol-low me!

Down Came a Bat
(Down Came a Lady)

Category

Action song (for Halloween)

Age

3 – 7

Equipment

None.

Formation

Ask the children to spread out and to sit on the floor.

Procedure

For this activity, the children should be familiar with the action song *Down Came a Lady*. Start by talking about bats with the children, show them a picture of a bat, and ask if any of them have actually seen a bat. Next sing the song to the children, and ask them what the bat is doing in the song. Then ask the children to demonstrate what type of arm movements a flying bat might use. Encourage the children to talk about their movements. Next, discuss how a bat uses a kind of radar when flying around; as the children move about the space, ask them to put on their "radar." (This will help them develop spatial awareness.) When the children are comfortable with their movements, sing the song as they perform.

Down Came a Bat

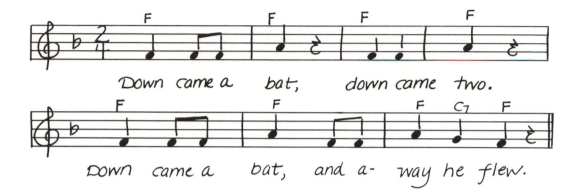

Down came a bat, down came two.

Down came a bat, and a-way he flew.

33

Down Came a Lady

Category

Action song

Age

3 – 7

Equipment

None.

Formation

Ask the children to stand so they are spread out about the area.

Procedure

Begin by suggesting that the children explore jumping in place. Start singing the song as the children continue their jumping movements. Next, ask for volunteers to demonstrate other movements that can be done with shoes on, such as walking in various ways, galloping, hopping. Encourage the children to talk about the ways they are moving. Then, with one of the volunteers acting as a leader and the others copying, sing the song, using either "lady" or "gentleman" and "her" or "his," depending on who is the leader. Change the song's wording to describe the new movement. For example, the last phrase might become "in her hopping shoes."

Variation

At first do the activity with just two children moving about the area, as mentioned in the song. This might be easier than having the entire class participate.

Down Came a Lady

Down came a lady, down came two

Down came a lady, in her jump-ing shoes.

Easter Song

(Here We Go Round the Mulberry Bush)

Category

Action song (seasonal)

Age

3 – 7

Equipment

None.

Formation

Ask the children to spread out about the activity area.

Procedure

Have the children explore "jumping" and "gathering eggs" before the song. Ask the children if there are other things the bunnies could do, and incorporate their suggestions in the song. As the children perform, ask them to describe the movements they are doing.

Easter Song

Traditional tune

This is the way the bun-nies jump,
bun-nies jump, bun-nies jump.
This is the way the bun-nies jump
on this Eas-ter day.

Verse 2: This is the way we gather
eggs, gather eggs, gather eggs.
Gather them high and gather
them low on this Easter day.

Eensy Weensy Spider

Category

Action song

Age

3 – 7

Equipment

None.

Formation

Ask the children to sit in an informal circle.

Procedure

Begin by having the children copy you as you raise your arms up high in front of your body while wiggling your fingers like a spider. Then bring your arms down with the fingers pointed down and without wiggling the fingers, and ask the children to copy. Next, ask them how the movement of "going up" was different from "going down." Now, ask the children to sequence those two movements, raising their arms with fingers wiggling and then bringing them down slowly with fingers pointing down and not wiggling. Repeat the two movements again, and sing the first part of the song along with these movements. (There is no movement for "washed the spider out.")

   After this, make the shape of the sun overhead with your arms, and ask the children to copy. Discuss the shape with them, and encourage them to comment on what it looks like to them. Now with fingers wiggling, repeat the movement, of "going up the waterspout." (There is no movement for "dried up all the rain.") Finally, sing the entire song while the children do the movements. Encourage the children to join in the singing when they are ready.

Eensy Weensy Spider

The een-sy ween-sy spi-der went up the wa-ter spout.

Down came the rain and washed the spi-der out.

Out came the sun and dried up all the rain, and the

een-sy, ween-sy spi-der went up the spout a-gain.

39

Everybody Pat With Jill
(Mary Had a Little Lamb)

Category

Action song

Age

3 – 7

Equipment

None.

Formation

Ask the children to sit in an informal circle.

Procedure

Ask the children to find different places on their bodies where they can pat the beat. Now ask for a volunteer to choose the place to pat the beat. Have all the children copy the volunteer's motion, and then begin the song to the children's beat. In the song, use the name of the child who is the leader. In addition to patting body parts, the children should try other movements that they all can do together, such as twisting and turning, walking, jumping, galloping, skipping.

Variations

Use the tune *Jimmy Crack Corn* and substitute the new words. Have the children "freeze" on the word "stop."

Everybody Pat With Jill

Traditional Tune

Ev-'ry-bod-y pat with Jill,

Pat with Jill, pat with Jill.

Ev-'ry-bod-y pat with Jill.

Who is our next lead-er?

* * * * * *

Tom-my pats his knees and so do we,

Tom-my pats his knees and so do we,

Tom-my pats his knees and so do we, And

now it's time to stop!

Follow Round the Kitchen
(All Around the Kitchen)

Category

Action song

Age

5 – 7

Equipment

None.

Formation

Ask the children to stand so they are spread out in a designated area.

Procedure

Tell the children that you are going to sing a song (which may also be used as a rhyme). Say "When you hear me say 'Follow round the kitchen,' please walk in place like this." Demonstrate walking in place. "When you hear me say 'stop,' what are you going to do?" After the children "freeze" in place, continue the activity by saying "Put your hands on your head. Put your hands on your shoes." Next, sing the song and ask the children to do the movements they have practiced. Join the children in the walking and stopping movement, but do not join them in touching head and shoes; instead, allow them to follow the verbal directions of the song without your demonstration.

Variations

• Suggest other places to pat. For example, say "Pat your hands on your shoulders . . ."

• Encourage a child to suggest a way to "follow round the kitchen." Use both the name of the child and the movement as you sing the song: "Can you hop like Mary, cock-a-doodle, doodle, doo? Follow round the kitchen, cock-a-doodle, doodle, doo." You might also suggest movements like twisting both arms or bending and straightening both knees. In each case, ask the children to try the new movement before beginning the song again.

Follow Round the Kitchen

Black American
Play song

Fol-low round the kit-chen, cock-a-doo-dle, doo-dle, doo. Fol-low

round the kit-chen, cock-a-doo-dle, doo-dle, doo. Now we

stop right here, cock-a- doo-dle, doo-dle, doo. Put your

hands on your head, cock-a-doo-dle, doo-dle, doo. Put your

hands on your shoe, cock-a-doo-dle, doo-dle, doo. Fol-low

round the kit-chen, cock-a- doo-dle, doo-dle doo. Fol-low

round the kit-chen, cock-a - doo-dle, doo-dle, doo.

43

Goin' Round the Circle
(Go Tell Aunt Rhody)

Category

Action song

Age

3 – 7

Equipment

None.

Formation

Ask the children to sit in an informal circle.

Procedure

Start by asking "Who would like to plan a way to travel around the circle? Mike, how are you going around the circle?" As Mike goes around the circle of seated children, suggest to the others that they each choose a movement to perform to a slow beat, such as rocking, or patting a body part as they remain seated. (In the song the words or syllables for the rock or pat are underlined.) As the children perform their movements and the volunteer circles, sing the song. Encourage the children to sing along with you as they begin to learn the song. When you finish the verse, the child who is circling should return to his or her place and a new volunteer should be chosen.

Variations

• The words of the song may be changed to incorporate the child's name, such as "Jimmy round the circle."

• The action the child has chosen may be incorporated instead: "Jump around the circle."

Goin' Round the Circle

Traditional Tune

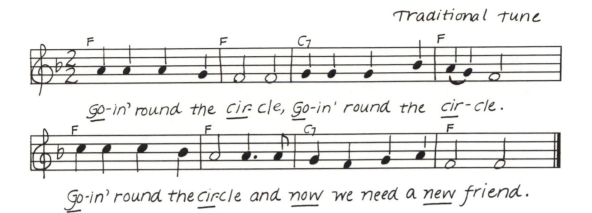

Go-in' round the cir-cle, Go-in' round the cir-cle.

Go-in' round the circle and now we need a new friend.

45

Jenny Mouse
(Paw Paw Patch)

Category

Action song

Age

3 – 7

Equipment

None.

Formation

Have the children sit in a circle.

Procedure

Ask the children for a volunteer who will plan and demonstrate a way of going around the circle (hopping, skipping, walking). Ask the others to plan a movement they can use to keep the beat. When singing the song, insert the name of the child who is going around the circle in place of "Jenny" and insert the chosen action in place of "go." For example, the group might sing, "Sarah Mouse, hop around the circle."

Jenny Mouse

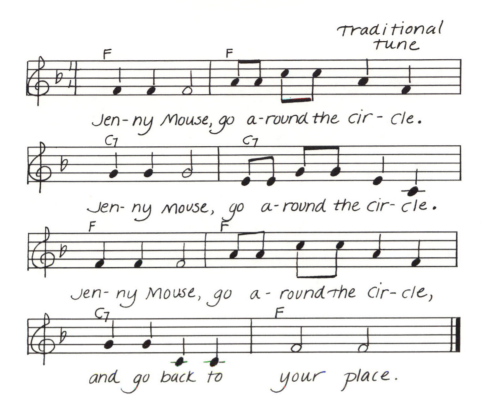

Traditional tune

Jen-ny Mouse, go a-round the cir-cle.

Jen-ny mouse, go a-round the cir-cle.

Jen-ny Mouse, go a-round the cir-cle,

and go back to your place.

Jungle Beat

Category

Action song (or rhyme)

Age

6 – 7

Equipment

A pair of rhythm sticks and a paper plate for each child.

Formation

Ask the children to sit in a circle.

Procedure

Ask the children to point to different body parts with rhythm sticks and then have them try tapping those body parts with the sticks. ("Point to your knees. Now tap your knees.") Have them explore the different sounds they can make as they tap the sticks together, or on the floor, or on a paper plate, or on their knees.

Ask one child to be the leader for the song and to select the way the others should tap their sticks. Then have the children use SAY & DO with the chosen movement. For example, while tapping the floor, they would say, "FLOOR, FLOOR, FLOOR." Finally, add the song (or rhyme) to the children's established beat.

Variations

• Have the children pat the beat with their hands on a stuffed animal or doll.

• Jungle Beat could become a counting song with the children choosing a different number and different animal. Thus "Two little monkeys" could become "Three little elephants." Then, when the verse is completed, have the children count out the number used in the verse.

• A child's name could be inserted in place of the words "Two little," so, "Two little monkeys" might become "Kevin monkey." Also insert the child's name in place of "Hey."

Jungle Beat

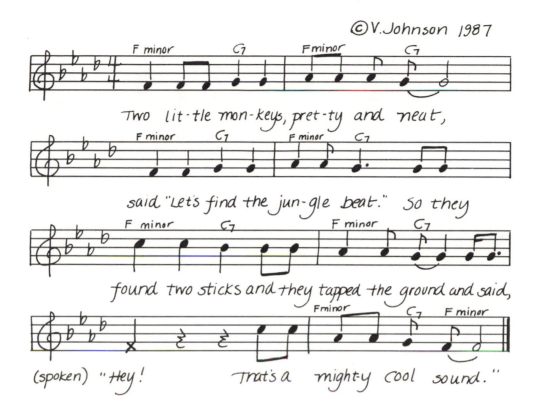

Two lit-tle mon-keys, pret-ty and neat,

said "Let's find the jun-gle beat." So they

found two sticks and they tapped the ground and said,

(spoken) "Hey!   That's a   might-y cool sound."

Little Red Wagon

(One Little, Two Little, Three Little Indians)

Category

Action song

Age

3 – 6

Equipment

None.

Formation

Ask the children to sit scattered about on the floor.

Procedure

While you are seated, jiggle up and down as though riding in a wagon. Ask "Can you jiggle your body the way I am jiggling mine?" When all are jiggling together, sing the song. Then ask, "What other way could we move in our wagon?" Suppose Martha would like to twist her body back and forth. Encourage all the children to try the suggested new movement. Then add the song, changing the words to "Martha says to twist in our little red wagon." Change the last line to "Who will be the next leader?" If children have difficulty thinking of other motions, you might suggest moving various body parts (using action words such as "shake," "thump").

Little Red Wagon

We're all here in the lit-tle red wag-on.

We're all here in the lit-tle red wag-on.

We're all here in the lit-tle red wag-on.

won't you be my good friend?

Old Man Mosie

Category

Action song (or rhyme)

Age

5 – 7

Equipment

A cane.

Formation

Ask the children to sit in an informal circle.

Procedure

Talk with the children about older people, and ask if they have seen an older person use a cane. After you demonstrate walking with a cane, ask different children to pretend they are older and to walk with the cane. Ask others to walk with a make-believe cane. Next talk about people who get sick and have to call the doctor. Ask children to pretend they are calling the doctor. Finally, sequence these two movements (walking with a cane and calling the doctor) and sing the first part of the song with the sequenced movements.

For the middle part of the song, have the children first practice stepping forward and turning around. Then have them add doing the Hokey Pokey as they turn. (The children should be familiar with the *Hokey Pokey* singing game before you introduce this activity.) Then add the corresponding words of the song to the motions. Finally, sequence these motions with the ones for the first part of the song. Then put the entire sequence together with the song.

For the last part of the song, talk about ways of getting out of town, such as crawling, walking, jumping. Have a volunteer choose a ''getting out of town'' movement for the other children to copy. For this movement, specify the pathway the children should follow, such as a pathway around the circle. Tell the children that at the song's end, you will count while they ''get out of town.''

Old Man Mosie

Old man Mos-ie sick in the head.

Called the doc-tor, the doc-tor said,

"Please step for-ward and turn a-round.

Do the Ho-key Po-key and get out of town!"

(SPOKEN) One, two, three, four, five, six, seven, eight!

One in a Boat
(Four in a Boat)

Category

Action song (modified version)

Age

3 – 7

Equipment

None.

Formation

Ask the children to sit scattered about the area.

Procedure

Begin by demonstrating a bending and straightening motion with your arms (like rowing a boat) and have the children copy. Then have them rock forward and backward. "Can you bend and straighten your arms while you rock forward and backward like this?" When the children are successful, start the song. The underlined words will help you set the beat for the rocking movement.

After the children are successful doing the movement individually, have them try the rocking motion while seated in pairs, facing each other. Each pair should join hands and move their arms back and forth while rocking. When the children are comfortable with the new movement, sing the song and sing "two in a boat" this time. Ask the children to think of other ways of rocking together, such as rocking from side to side.

Try the movement with larger boats — three or more children sitting one behind the other, and adapt the words to the number of children. Children may also sit side by side in the boat and rock and row that way. Change the numbers in the song to fit the situation in the boat.

One in a Boat

Pizza Hut

(A Ram Sam Sam)

Category

Action song (variation)

Age

3 – 7

Equipment

None.

Formation

Have the children sit in an informal circle.

Procedure

Have the children copy the way you make a circle (a pizza shape) with both arms. To make the circle, both arms should be held in front of the body, with just finger-tips touching. Then have them copy putting both arms overhead with palms touching (to make the shape of a hut). You might ask them to talk about the differences between the two movements. Next demonstrate how to sequence the two movements. Finally, sing the words "Pizza Hut! Pizza Hut!" while repeating this sequence twice; this is the beginning of the song.

For the next phrase of the song, have the children copy the way you flap your upper arms against your body (like a chicken). Practice flapping arms four times and then doing the Pizza Hut movement once. With this sequence of movements, sing "Kentucky Fried Chicken and a Pizza Hut."

For the phrase "McDonald's," show children the new movement of raising both pointing fingers up in an arch and then putting them down again (to simulate the McDonald's arch). Do this movement twice while singing "McDonald's, McDonald's."

Pizza Hut

Rock-A-Bye, Baby

Category

Action song

Age

3 – 4

Equipment

None.

Formation

Ask the children to be seated on the floor in a scattered fashion.

Procedure

Begin by having the children explore different ways to rock their bodies. Encourage different children to demonstrate for the others the ways they are moving and to talk about their movement. Draw attention to specific children by saying "Is Jose rocking fast or slow? Is it a quiet rocking or a noisy rocking? Let's copy Jose." Once the children are all moving together, add the song. The underlined words or syllables should match the rocking beat. Repeat, with another child as the leader, and encourage the children to join in the song.

Variations

• Each child might hold and rock a stuffed animal or doll, or the child who is leader might do so. The teacher might hold a child and rock with that child while the others hold their animal or doll friends.

• Older children may enjoy rocking together as partners. To do this, two partners can sit inside a hula hoop or both hold a hoop. Have them plan the way they are going to rock together.

• Have the entire group sit in a long line and together rock back and forth or from side to side.

Rock-A-Bye, Baby

Traditional tune

Rock-a-bye, ba-by, on the tree top.
when the wind blows, the cra-dle will rock.
when the bough breaks, the cra-dle will fall, and
down will come ba-by, cra-dle and all.

Rockin' in the Boat

Category

Action song

Age

3 – 7

Equipment

A stuffed animal for each child (optional).

Formation

Ask the children to sit in an informal circle or scattered about the area.

Procedure

Encourage the children to copy you as you rock forward and back to a steady beat. Say "Can you do what I'm doing? We call this rocking. Let's all rock together." Then sing the song to the rocking beat the children are using. The forward rock should occur on each underlined word (two forward- and -back rocks, or two beats, to a measure).

Variations

• A child can sit in the lap of an older child or adult and be rocked to the song, or an older child can kneel behind a younger child and place hands on the upper arms of the seated child to rock that child from side to side.

• Have the children explore other movements, such as patting some part of the body, shaking both hands, or tapping toes. Vary the song to suit the patting, shaking, or tapping beat established by the group. For example, sing "See me shake my hands and the tide rolls high." This beat can be a quicker beat, four beats for each measure of the song.

• As the children become more experienced, have them rock forward two times to each measure (on the underlined words) and simultaneously pat a part of the body (four pats to each measure).

Rockin' in the Boat

Traditional tune

Rock-in' in the boat and the tide rolls high,

Rock-in' in the boat and the tide rolls high,

Rock-in' in the boat and the tide rolls high,

See me rock my boat as I rock by'n by.

Shake Our Bells

(Jingle Bells)

Category

Action song (holiday or seasonal)

Age

3 – 5

Equipment

One or two bells for each child.

Formation

Ask the children to sit in an informal circle.

Procedure

Begin by having the children explore a bell-ringing (shaking) motion with each hand, if they haven't done this before. After they shake one hand, suggest they try it with the other hand. Also, if some children have two bells, ask them to practice shaking both hands at once. Ask a child to be the leader and to show everyone a way to shake the bells during the song. Then use that child's name in the song.

Variations

This action song may be used as a Valentine's Day song by substituting the following words:

Beating hearts, beating hearts, beating steadily,
Pat the beat on your special heart, on this Valentine's Day.

Put a cut-out heart on the floor in front of each child and have them pat the beat on their cut-out hearts while the song is sung.

Shake Our Bells

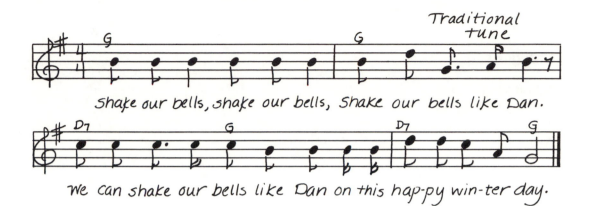

shake our bells, shake our bells, Shake our bells like Dan.

We can shake our bells like Dan on this hap-py win-ter day.

63

Shape Song
(Here We Go Round the Mulberry Bush)

Category

Action song

Age

3 – 7

Equipment

A carpet square or hula hoop for each child.

Formation

Have each child stand on a carpet square or inside a hula hoop.

Procedure

Strike a statue pose for the children to copy and then sing the song, substituting your name for "Phyllis." At the end of the song ask facilitating questions, such as "Where are my hands? Are they up high or down low? Are my feet far apart or close together?" By asking questions, you help the children to more accurately perceive the shape you are making with your body. Have a child volunteer to "make the next statue shape" while the song is sung, and then have the children copy. Again ask questions regarding the pose (or shape).

Variations

• With older children, you may want to have them strike a pose with one body part moving, such as a hand waving or a head nodding.

• You may wish to specify a basic position the children must stay in while making their statue shape, such as sitting, kneeling, or lying down.

Shape Song

Traditional tune

This is the shape that Phyl-lis makes,

Phyl-lis makes, Phyl-lis makes.

This is the shape that Phyl-lis makes.

Let's all make the same shape.

Someone's in the Center

Category

Action song

Age

3 – 7

Equipment

None.

Formation

Have the children stand in an informal circle.

Procedure

Ask a child to volunteer to be the leader. The leader may want to stand in the center of the circle. Have this leader do a repetitive movement that the others can copy. You may first need to model such a movement, for example, leaping back and forth from one foot to the other. After the children have all started to do the movement, begin the song. Sing to match the beat of the leader's movement and sing the leader's name in place of "Tommy." Other children can then volunteer to be the next leader.

Someone's in the Center

Some-one is the lead-er. Tom-my is his name.

Ev-'ry-thing that he does, we'll do the same.

Statue Shapes

(The Farmer in the Dell)

Category

Action song

Age

4 – 7

Equipment

None.

Formation

Ask the children to stand so they are scattered about the area.

Procedure

Have the children explore making statue shapes. When the children are "frozen" in a shape, sing the song. When you sing the second verse, have the children change their shapes. For the third verse, have the children explore moving some part of their statue (for example, both arms) to the beat. For the fourth verse, have the children explore moving their statues about the space. Before singing each verse, explain what the children are to do and have them plan what they will do when the verse is being sung.

Statue Shapes

We make a stat-ue shape. We make a stat-ue shape.

Hi! Ho! the der-ry O! We make a stat-ue shape.

Verse 2: We change our statue shape. (2 times)
       Hi! Ho! The derry O! We change our statue shape.
Verse 3: Our statues move in beat. (2 times)
       Hi! Ho! The derry O! Our statues move in beat.
Verse 4: Our statues move around. (2 times)
       Hi! Ho! The derry O! Our statues move around.

Teddy Bear

Category

Action song

Age

3 – 6

Equipment

A teddy bear for each child.

Formation

Have the children sit in a circle with teddy bears on their laps.

Procedure

Have the children explore ways that they can make a teddy bear pat various parts of its body or "walk" its feet. Ask a child volunteer to be the leader and to choose a part of the body for all the teddy bears to pat together. Then have all the children practice this patting movement with their bears, using SAY & DO. For example, they might make the bears pat their knees and chant "KNEES, KNEES, KNEES, KNEES" as the bears pat. After this practice, have the child leader begin the patting movement. As the others join in, add the song to the activity. The beat of the song should match the beat the children have established. If the walking movement is selected, practice with the SAY & DO of "WALK, WALK, WALK, WALK."

Variation

Substitute Care Bears or baby dolls for the teddy bears. Replace the words "Teddy Bear" with appropriate words.

Teddy Bear

Black American

Ted-dy Bear, Ted-dy Bear pats his knees.

Ted-dy Bear, Ted-dy Bear pats his knees.

Ted-dy Bear, Ted-dy Bear pats his knees.

Ted-dy Bear, Ted-dy Bear, hug me please.

Three Little Children
(Three Blue Pigeons)

Category

Action song

Age

5 – 7

Equipment

A large block for each child to use as a "wall."

Formation

Have the children stand scattered around the area.

Procedure

Ask the children to move about the room in different pathways — straight, curved, and zigzag. Remind them not to touch one another. Ask "What kind of pathway did you take? How did you travel?" (*Note.* We're assuming that children have explored pathways prior to introducing this activity and that they understand the terminology.) Then say "This time, when you move in your pathways, I will say 'freeze.' This will mean to stop like a statue. Now let's all start to move." After the children begin to move, say "Freeze. Were you able to freeze like a statue but not fall down?" Encourage the children to describe their statues. Ask such questions as "Where are your statue's arms? What parts of your statue's body are touching the floor?"

To introduce the song about three little children sitting on a wall, have the children form into groups of three, with each child in the group seated on a block, which is the "wall." Have each group decide who will be the first, second, or third child to "fly away." Ask the first child in each group "What pathway are you going to use as you move? What am I going to say when I want you to stop like a statue? What will you do when you stop?" Then ask all the "first" children to move and then tell them to "freeze." Next ask the "second" child in each group how he or she plans to move in a pathway, and repeat the process of having these children move and "freeze." Do the same with the "third" children. Finally, have the children return to their starting places in the same (first, second, and third) order. After the children have practiced the movement in this way, begin the song. Before adding each new verse, ask the children how many children are left sitting on the wall.

Three Little Children

Traditional tune

Three lit-tle chil-dren sitting on the wall,

Three lit-tle chil-dren sit-ting on the wall.

(spoken by one person) One of them flew away
           (All-sadly) O-o-o-oh!

Verse 2: Two little children sitting on the wall,
           (Spoken) Another child flew away.
           (All-more sadly) O-o-o-o-o!

Verse 3: One little child sitting on the wall,
           (Spoken) And the third one flew away!
           (All) O-o-o-o-o-o-o-o!

Verse 4: No little children sitting on the wall,
           (Spoken) One of the children came back.
           (All) Wheee!

Verse 5: One little child sitting on the wall,
           (Spoken) Another flew back!
           (All) Wheeeeeee!

Verse 6: Two little children sitting on the wall,
           (spoken) And the third one came back!
           (All) Wheeeeeeeeeeee!

Verse 7: Three little children sitting on the wall!
           (Spoken) There's nothing more to say!

Where Is Thumbkin?

Category

Action song

Age

3 – 7

Equipment

None.

Formation

Have the children sit scattered about the space or in an informal circle.

Procedure

Demonstrate and ask children to copy a movement in which you put both hands behind your back. Then bring both hands in front with the thumbs up and have the children copy. After trying this several times, show the children how to bring only one hand out in front at a time. Then introduce the first part of the song, first putting your hands behind your back and then bringing out one hand at a time with each "Here I am."

Next ask "Can you make your thumbs talk to each other like this?" Demonstrate wiggling your thumbs at each other and have the children copy. Then ask "Can you make one thumb talk first and then have the other one answer?" Show how to wiggle first one, then the other thumb, and have the children copy. It should be noted that not many children will be able to hold one thumb still while moving the other, so don't expect mastery. For the words "Run away," show children how to make one thumb, and then the other, go behind the back. The entire song may then be added to the movements.

Where Is Thumbkin?

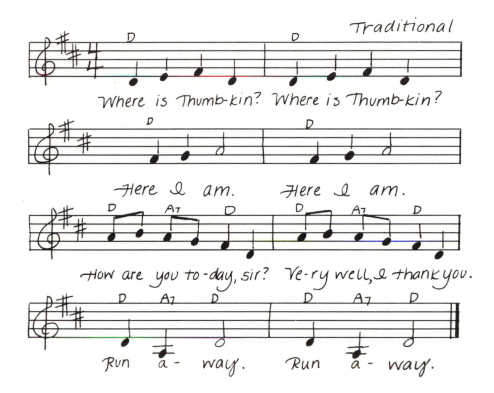

Where is Thumb-kin? Where is Thumb-kin?

Here I am. Here I am.

How are you to-day, sir? Ve-ry well, I thank you.

Run a - way. Run a - way.

Where, Oh, Where Have Our Furry Friends Gone?

(Where, Oh, Where Has My Little Dog Gone?)

Category

Action song

Age

3 – 6

Equipment

A "furry friend" (stuffed animal) for each child.

Formation

Have the children sit scattered around the area, each holding an animal.

Procedure

Have the children hide their furry friends somewhere on or around themselves. Discuss where their friends are hiding. Then have them *plan* where they will hide the furry friends next, and then move them to this new hiding place. After they have hidden the animals a second time, sing the song and ask the children to pat or rock to the beat of the song. After the song is sung, talk about where the animals have been hidden.

Next, have one child hide his or her stuffed animal somewhere in the room. Change the words of the song accordingly: "Oh, where, oh, where has Nathan's panda gone?" After the song is over, Nathan can describe where he put the panda, or the other children may try to find the panda.

Where, Oh, Where Have Our Furry Friends Gone?

Singing Games

Draw a Bucket of Water

Category

Singing game (traditional movement simplified)

Age

3 – 7

Equipment

A piece of tape (on the floor), or a hula hoop, for each child.

Formation

Have the children stand scattered about the area, each in a designated place, such as on the tape placed on the floor or inside a hula hoop.

Procedure

Demonstrate for the children a movement that consists of pushing both arms out in front of the body and then pulling them back towards the body. Then have the children do the movement. The movement should be explored using both arms at once and also explored alternating right and left arms. Encourage the children to talk about the movement, what their arms are doing, how it feels, and so on.

Next show a movement in which you stand and bend both knees, saying "I'm sinking lower." Then straighten your knees and rise up on your toes and say "Now I'm rising higher." Have the children practice sinking lower and rising higher. Also have the children jump in place.

After all these movements have been practiced, sing the song while the children do the movements. On the first line, the children move both arms away and then towards the body two times. On the second line, which is spoken, they do the same movement (away and towards), but with alternate arms, and they do the movement twice as fast as they did it for the first line. On the third line they bend and then straighten their knees. On the fourth line, which is spoken, they jump up and down two times with each set of "jump, jump."

Variation

Once the children are comfortable with the singing game, they can try performing it in pairs. In each pair, the partners should face each other and hold hands. Be certain to stress that partners should be careful in pushing and pulling each other's arms.

Draw a Bucket of Water

Traditional tune

Draw a buc-ket of wa-ter for my la-dy's daugh-ter.

(spoken) One in a rush, two in a rush, three in a rush, four in a rush.

I'm sink-ing low-er. I'm ris-ing high-er.

(spoken) Jump in the wa-ter, jump, jump. Jump in the wa-ter, jump, jump.

The Farmer in the Dell

Category

Singing game (traditional movement modified)

Age

5 – 7

Equipment

None.

Formation

Ask the children to stand scattered about the area.

Procedure

Have the children explore different ways of moving around the room. Each child should choose a body part, such as the nose or elbow, to "lead" in the movement. Have them talk about the ways they are moving.

Divide the class into five groups. Each group will represent one of the characters in the song, such as the farmer, the wife, and so on, and that group should decide what nonlocomotor or locomotor movement they will perform when their verse of the song is sung. Have each group demonstrate their chosen movement before beginning the song. Encourage the children to move with the beat of the song.

Variation

Older children can first do the singing game described above. Then one farmer (from the farmer group) chooses a wife (from the wife group) and the two move while attached together in some way. Next they choose a child, and the three of them become attached and move together, and so on. At the end of the song, the five attached children (farmer, wife, child, nurse, dog) freeze into a "statue." The activity can continue with a new farmer choosing a wife, and so on. Continue until all children have had a turn. You might wish to add a final verse: "The statues start to move. . . ." The children should find a way to move to the beat while they are attached.

The Farmer in the Dell

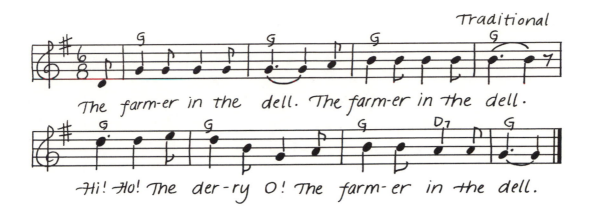

The farm-er in the dell. The farm-er in the dell.

Hi! Ho! The der-ry O! The farm-er in the dell.

Verse 2: The farmer takes a wife...
Verse 3: The wife takes a child...
Verse 4: The child takes a nurse...
Verse 5: The nurse takes a dog...

Hokey Pokey

Category

Singing game

Age

3 – 7

Equipment

None.

Formation

Have the children stand in an informal circle.

Procedure

Have the children copy your motion of putting both hands in toward the center of the circle. Then have them copy putting both hands out of the circle. Repeat that motion several times and ask the children to describe where their arms are moving. Label the movements "in" and "out," saying "Put your two hands in. Put them out. Put them in again." Next show the shaking motion. Sequence the first four movements, (hands in, out, in again, and shaking all about) and then accompany those movements with the first two lines of the song.

To prepare for the last two lines of the song, have the children turn all the way around and then try turning again in a "funny" way. Explain that this turning around in a funny way is called "doing the Hokey Pokey." Next demonstrate the Hokey Pokey turning movement while singing the corresponding line of the song and have the children join in. Finally, add the last movement, which is four slow pats of the legs, and with this movement, sing "That's what it's all about." The whole singing game may then be put together. Encourage the children to join in the song when they feel ready.

If it seems appropriate to continue with other verses, say "Who can think of some other part of the body that we can put in and out? Yolanda says we should put one arm in. Let's try that." As you add each new verse, be certain to have the children try the movement before singing the verse. Use the words "one side" and "other side" rather than "right" and "left."

Variation

Have the children hold an object, such as a stuffed animal or a block, and do the singing game using the object. For example, a child's teddy bear might put two hands in, put two hands out, and so on.

Hokey Pokey

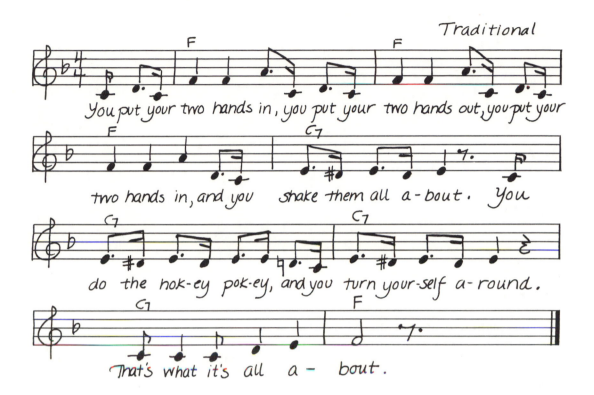

Traditional

You put your two hands in, you put your two hands out, you put your two hands in, and you shake them all a-bout. You do the hok-ey pok-ey, and you turn your-self a-round. That's what it's all a-bout.

Let Everyone Move With Me

Category

Singing game

Age

3 – 7

Equipment

None.

Formation

Ask the children to stand scattered about the activity area.

Procedure

Help the children explore various ways to perform nonlocomotor and locomotor movements. Ask for a child volunteer to be the leader in doing a movement for others to copy. Have the other children follow the leader and describe the movement they are doing. Then add the song to the leader's movement, and in place of "me" in the song, use the name of the child who is the leader. If the leader is using a movement that can be labeled (such as marching, swinging, shaking) use that word for the word "move" in the song (for example, "Let every one march with Paul").

Variations

● Have the children touch one body part and then another, in a two-motion sequence. Say the parts of the body as they are touched, such as "KNEES, SHOULDERS." Once the group is moving together, add the song, doing this movement sequence to the beat of the song.

● If the children are older or more experienced, you may wish to have one child after the other be the leader, until all have had a turn. Signal each child's turn by saying "Show us your movement. You are next." After the child shows the new movement, begin the song again, with everyone copying the new movement.

Let Everyone Move With Me

Folk song

Let ev'-ry one move with me. Let ev'-ry one move with me. Come on and join in-to the game. You'll find that it's al-ways the same!

Old King Glory

Category

Singing game (modified version)

Age

3 – 7

Equipment

None.

Formation

Have the children sit in an informal circle.

Procedure

With both hands, begin to pat your knees to a steady beat and encourage the children to join in. When all are patting together, sing the song. Ask for a volunteer to sit in the middle of the circle and to lead the beat with a different movement, such as patting both shoulders or shaking both hands. Then ask for a volunteer to be Old King Glory and to move around the outside of the circle. Before the song begins, Old King Glory should plan the way he is going to move around the outside of the circle. Substitute the name of the child for ''Glory'' and substitute ''Queen'' for ''King,'' if necessary (for example, sing ''Old Queen Tammy of the mountain . . .''). You might wish to put a crown on the head of the king (or queen) and to give the leader in the middle of the circle something special to wear.

Variation

Children in kindergarten or first grade may use a more complicated version in which Old King Glory touches the shoulders of three different children when everyone sings ''The first one, the second one, the third follow me.'' Those who are touched should get up and follow Old King Glory, copying the way he is moving. Each time the song is sung, choose a new volunteer to lead the beat movement and a new volunteer to be king or queen.

Old King Glory

Old King Glo-ry of the moun-tain. The
moun-tain was so high, it near-ly touched the sky. The
first one, the sec-ond one, the third fol-low me.

Pass the Beanbag, Tideo

(Jingle at the Window)

Category

Singing game (modified version)

Age

6 – 7

Equipment

A beanbag for each child (yarnballs or small teddy bears may be used instead).

Formation

Have the children sit in an informal circle.

Procedure

Ask the children to pretend that they are holding imaginary beanbags in both hands on the floor in front of them. Show the children how to pass an imaginary beanbag to the next child. They should move both hands to the floor in front of the next child and then return both hands to the floor in front of themselves. The words "PASS, WAIT" can be added as the children practice. On the word "PASS," the children should pass the imaginary beanbag to the next child, and on the word "WAIT," they should take hold of the imaginary beanbag that has been passed to them. You or one of the children can set the beat. Tell the children that they will hear the word "pass" in the song that you will sing; they should pass the imaginary beanbag every time you sing that word. When they are successful passing an imaginary beanbag, add real beanbags. With the real beanbags, first have them chant the words "PASS, WAIT" and then have them respond to the song. Be certain to have the children practice passing to the left as well as to the right, though you need not use those directional words.

Variations

- Have children try passing beanbags with one hand.

- For older children, have them toss the beanbags up in the air and then catch the beanbag. Change the lyrics as follows:

  Toss and catch it, ti-de-o. (3 times)
  Toss it up and catch it, ti-de-o.
  Ti-de-o, ti-de-o, toss it up and catch it, ti-de-o.

- For younger children, insert the word "DROP" for the word "PASS" and "PICK IT UP" for "WAIT." Have the children drop the beanbag in front of themselves and then pick it up again. The lyrics then change as follows:

  Drop the beanbag, ti-de-o. (3 times)
  Drop it on the floor, ti-de-o.
  Ti-de-o, ti-de-o, drop it on the floor, ti-de-o.

Pass the Beanbag, Tideo

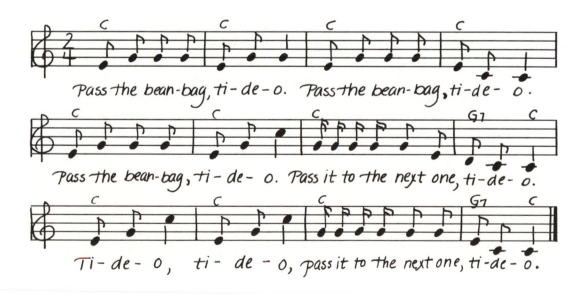

91

Punchinello

Category

Singing game (modified version)

Age

5 – 7

Equipment

A stuffed monkey for the teacher to hold.

Formation

Have the children sit in an informal circle.

Procedure

While you hold the monkey and sway from side to side with it, have everyone sway from side to side slowly. Sing or chant the first verse of the song, matching the swaying beat the children are using (the underlined words indicate the steady beat).

Next, ask "What part of his body shall we have our funny monkey pat?" Suppose the children select the ears. Then sway the monkey and make it pat its ears during the second verse, while the children continue to sway from side to side.

Finally, have the children practice patting their own ears and then add the third verse. Encourage the children to continue swaying while they pat.

Punchinello

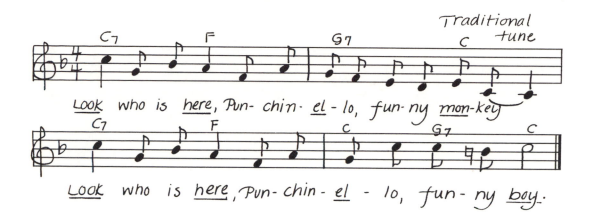

Traditional tune

Look who is here, Pun-chin-el-lo, fun-ny mon-key

Look who is here, Pun-chin-el-lo, fun-ny boy.

Verse 2: What can you do, Punchinello, funny monkey?
          What can you do, Punchinello, funny boy?
Verse 3: We can do it too, Punchinello, funny monkey.
          We can do it too, Punchinello, funny boy.

Notes

Notes

Notes